ten acres of the universe

poems
Paul Bowers

Copyright © 2022 Paul Bowers
All Rights Reserved

Book Design: Rowan Kehn
ISBN: 978-1-7355762-5-1

Turning Plow Press

As always, for Denise and Sydney

and for Mom and Dad
Claudette Bowers (1931-2012)
and
E.C. Bowers, Jr. (1931-2020)

Acknowledgments

Some of these poems appeared in *Dragon Poet Review* and the anthology *Bull Buffalo and Indian Paint Brush: The Poetry of Oklahoma*.

Special thanks to my fellow poets Roy Beckemeyer, Alan Berecka, Ken Hada, and Don Stinson for their invaluable feedback, and to Rowan Kehn, who puts it all together.

Contents

I   when singing time comes

On Witnessing a Farmer Plowing a New Field in Spring, Major Co., Oklahoma	3
Yellow	4
Venus and Jupiter in Close Proximity	5
Fallen	6
A Lesson in Botany	7
In This Jerusalem	8
The Mare I Buried Six Years Ago	9
The Seventh Day	10
Migration	11
Fourteen Lines in Spring	12
The Flood	13
Special of the Day	14
A Squirrel Comes to My Porch	15
Sunday Morning Encounter with Turkeys	16

II   summer fables

A Summer Fable	19
When I Dope the Pony	20
At the Museum in August	21
Old Riding Mower, and *Epiphaneia*	22
White Heron at the Farm Pond	23
At the Checkout Line	25
I Question the Moral Order of the Cosmos	26
East Side Son	27
Patients	29
Grackles at the Stoplight	30

III   this late in harvest time

September Matins	33

Testing Protagoras	34
6 AM	35
My Mother's Revision	36
Feeding My Mother an Enchilada	37
On My 58th Birthday	38
Running in the Dark	39
Late Harvest	41

IV   the long winter of memory

Origin Story	45
Two Photos	46
In the Pocket of My Winter Coat	47
Spooky Action at a Distance	48
Drinking Beer and Writing Poetry	49
Body and Soul	50
Birthdays There	51
December	52
Season's Greetings	53
The Sky Rests in Pure Blue Thought	54
Formal Complaint	55
Elegy for Donald Hall	56
The Making of Poetry	57
On My Father Dying Behind Hospital Glass	59
Osteomancy	60
My Neighbor Tells Me About Losing Her Father	61
Driving by Our Old, Abandoned House	62
A Short Bucket List of Impossible Things	63
Golden-tongued	64
Nearly There	65
County Road 48	66
After the Storm	67

To see a World in a Grain of Sand
And a Heaven in a Wild Flower
Hold Infinity in the palm of your hand
And Eternity in an hour

———

William Blake
Auguries of Innocence

I

when singing time comes

On Witnessing a Farmer Plowing a New Field in Spring, Major Co., Oklahoma

How you scribe the earth
how you slow its spin by increments
how you gouge the past
and roil it up again

that ragged history in soil
those remembrances of rain
and drought, eons only inches deep

speaking in rows of curling hillocks
a rope of clenched fists
and mounded beliefs

that score of knotted notes
played by an iron needle
when singing time comes.

Yellow

When February lets go
and March makes up its mind
the bees wear pants of pollen
their honey-dipped legs
furred in yellow

yellow as the shag carpet we rolled on as kids
when we opened the door to our new house in Oklahoma,
1972, when Nixon was president, and Vietnam almost over.
It was the day before the furniture arrived
so lots of space to tumble an afternoon away.

Sometimes our elbows or knees barely brushed another's
wing-like, before we careened off
to other rooms, to more distant meadows.

Venus and Jupiter in Close Proximity

Jupiter hangs bright, but night-weary
around the neck and shoulders of Venus.
They are the last two dancers at the dance
the only couple left on the dance floor
of the morning sky, all the other planets
and stars and galaxies long exhausted
dim-witted, and heading home at dawn
the dying glow of their headlights
disappearing over the farthest hilltop of the Milky Way.
The sun, father-like, threatens arrival at any minute
to untangle the couple and take his daughter home.
Mother is already in bed, curled into a crescent moon
waning but restless, aware of the powerful pull
of love, no matter how distant their bodies
may eventually be when day comes
and sends them into their separate orbits.
She remembers that heft of falling bodies
always falling inward toward one another
in their vast but narrowing ellipses.

Fallen

The third clutch of phoebes shed one casualty
a naked dollop we found on the porch.
The dog found it first, sniffed at the lollipop body
until my daughter pushed him away.

The nest
a bowl of earth and horsehair clinging to the porch lintel
had birthed nine chicks since spring began.

How this last one came to fall we couldn't know
but my daughter picked it up and held it lovingly
in her palm

a still, pink cherub ejected from on high

a featherless fall akin to flight
but only akin
only like.

A Lesson in Botany

I asked you
what are those flowers that grow
in a great bulbous knot

like irregular balloons
of off-white

with smaller blooms
that make a colony
like coral

the kind that gets heavy
in summer
like disappointment

and bows
to the ground
worshipful of its own roots

the kind bees love so much
they fly from one
to another

kissing each
and every blossom?

You said, *Hydrangeas*,
which, in the language of flowers
means gratitude.

Now I know what name they go by
and the secret word bees hum in the petals.

In This Jerusalem

In this Jerusalem
horses on pilgrimage

move along pasture paths
travel morning
and evening—

the ritual of the narrow gate
the way to and from

grasses chrismed with dew
to the farthest hilltop.

Along its crest
a sepulcher of flayed trees

Zion in spring
Gethsemane in fall
Golgotha in winter.

Mid-day the horses
hidden by distance
are silent in the hollow.

At sunset, like a prophet of old,
I whistle a proclamation
and watch the horizon
for their sudden return.

The Mare I Buried Six Years Ago

Badgers tunnel
        inside her hollow frame

knit her white coat
        into pillow cases

her ribs
        a beamed bedroom

her hooves
        decorative doorstops

her eyes
        enameled portholes

her whiskered chin
        a welcome mat.

The Seventh Day

Today was not a work day
in favor of letting the birds
sing to us of a Sunday morning.

So of course we built a wooden deck.
We laid mulch
and arranged a stone border.

We hammered like maddened woodpeckers
we organized like hopeful bowerbirds
and bickered like blue jays.

Before we know it, it is Sunday evening.
The birds abandon the sky
and fold their songs like wings.

We press our sore palms together
in the coming dark
our vespers prayers rough as skin.

Migration

Sandhill cranes
        sing their high hymns
        trilling the sky
on pilgrimage to Platte River

itinerate saints
        come to minister to us
        for three Sunday mornings
like squabbling preachers in a raucous revival

whose message is March and April
        and the blessings of miles
        travelled in chorus.
Praise what is above us.

Fourteen Lines in Spring

Currying a white horse in April
is like skinning an angel.

The white mare
hitches her hip

one back hoof tipped at ease
to show she is certain in her belief.

The sorrel gelding
also sheds his winter coat

and each comb's stroke
litters the ground with strands

of December's rust, like old wire.
He is less certain of warmer days, though,

faithlessly shifts his weight
left, then right.

The Flood

Water rose to the hips of memory
sat in the rocking chair
where my mother once rocked me
reclined on the old couch cushions
fingered the surprised electrical outlets
set the lonely goldfish free
found my father's worn work boots
and untied the laces.
The river crept into my sister's closet
tried on her skirts and roller skates.
Out back the laying hens
had danced briefly on the brittle surface, then turned
miraculously into feathered fish and travelled downstream.
(A week later I gathered their last eggs from the soggy henhouse
and flung them as offerings to the east.)
The kitchen table where we ate for years
stood on unsure legs; aging kitchen chairs
overturned and nervous in their sodden bones.

On the coffee table warped as a hammock
a ceramic mug full of river water
the cooled drink of a guest who came to visit
chatted about the rainy weather
then without so much as a wave
slid from my mother's rocking chair
and out the open door.

We hope he will not visit us again,
to steal so unneighborly in and out of that house
and the past we no longer live in.

Special of the Day

Today Christ is
King of ings
the lettered sign reads
outside Swadley's Barbecue.

Even Jesus, pitchman
for sweet red sauce and cloyed ribs
can't hang forever
on that slotted board

so he dropped a letter
as if to let go one finger
and gain some small release.

A Squirrel Comes to My Porch

I caught sight
of the spindled tail.

That's all.
But the yellow daffodils

in the border bed
waved familiarly

in the wind
to the whole of him—

Sunday Morning Encounter with Turkeys

They look like a Baptist choir taking
the stage in a hurry

dark robes fluttering
wings wild with the messages

they carry
on sheet music

tucked inside their sleeves.
When we edge closer

they transform
into a running chorus

and teach us
in their swaying motions

lessons in ecstatic worship
on this broad, lonely field

before the final flying aria
and their rising exit

over the tree-line
scattering whole notes of praise:

leaving us, their silent congregation,
blessed, but behind.

II

summer fables

A Summer Fable

The dog startles a snake
from the shadowy leaves
of the vegetable garden

then loses sight of it
in the surrounding taller grass.
I call him back to me.

Suddenly a summer rabbit
sleek and spring-loaded
braves the open space

jumps, twists, drums its feet
and banishes the mottled snake
to the horse pasture.

Somewhere in the nearby brush pile
there must be little ones
worthy of defense.

The moral of the story comes
when the rabbit pauses
looks past its ears at the two of us

me and the disappointed dog
who wait on the sidelines, wondering
how to enter into such life.

When I Dope the Pony

Because he won't stand still for the farrier
I syringe a sedative under the pony's tongue.

Thirty minutes later
he stands with his head hung low

sways left and right
like a tethered barrel of water in a slow-moving truck

clicks his tongue, tastes the sleep that creeps
from mouth to throat to vein to spine to muscle

soon feels a spirit walk a slow circle
around his body, lifting one hoof after another.

When he comes to, he is alone
a blue bucket of fresh water close by, a sheaf of clean hay

nearer the familiar world of barn and pasture
but also, somehow, knowing there is more.

At the Museum in August

She went to the art museum
Without a scarf
Without hoop earrings

He went in cut-off jeans
And red suspenders

The twins went with their tired mother who promised ice cream

Old lady Brentwood went by herself with a sandwich in her purse
And stood in front of two girls in a Renoir.
Both wore hats, and glowed

The attendant, all in funeral black
Walked 14 miles between Picassos
There and back, there
And back

Lastly, I took a photo of a man staring at a blank white wall
Marveling at what he saw.

Old Riding Mower, and *Epiphaneia*

So I drained and refilled the gas tank
then replaced the ignition coil
then the spark plugs
then disconnected the safety kill switch
then tested the valve compression
tightened and re-gapped the push arms
used starter fluid
rebuilt the carb—

but still it wouldn't start.

Finally, in despair, I aired
up the worn tires
gently wiped down the dented engine hood
polished the cracked seat
shined the loose steering wheel
in preparation for a trip
somewhere, maybe
to the scrap yard.

I thought, as well, about how my father had grown so old
       and used a cane and fiddled with his hearing aids
       and never wore a suit anymore.

White Heron at the Farm Pond

A Master in the Akaishi Mountains
folded a white paper heron
and launched it from Mt. Shiomi:
a slow glide down 10,000 feet
then 6,000 miles across the Pacific
over the northern climes

arcing above San Francisco
blown over Death Valley, Las Vegas
Tuba City, Santa Fe
then swirling north of Amarillo
to catch a living updraft in Boise City
before settling almost weightless
on the rim of my shallow pond in Oklahoma—

a pond that will dry and fracture come July
leaving the bird brittle, time-stained
and longing for the nimble fingers
of its maker, centuries absent from the peak
of that distant, holy mountain.

At the Checkout Line

We paused to let the man through
to the checker. We pushed a cart
full of cans, cartons, vegetables,
loose fruits. He had two frozen somethings,
microwave-ready, and could hardly believe his luck.

He smiled when my wife waved him forward
as if such small acts coaxed the soul
nearer the skin's surface, and once there,
took a long quiet breath, exhaled, waved back.

I Question the Moral Order of the Cosmos

If as Dante relates
the bottom of Hell
being furthest from God
is locked in ice

July in Oklahoma
must be Heaven
which makes
no damned sense.

East Side Son

You
with your leaning largemouth bass mailbox
and six terracotta pots
with no plants and no soil

You
with a dead push mower buried
in a jungle lawn

You
who sit on the porch barefoot
hair a disconnected robin's nest
in your Batman pajama bottoms
smoking a cigarette

You
who go to yard sales
and buy the stuff you sold
at your yard sale
but get it back at a real bargain

You
who carry a big stick
to walk your dog
through the neighborhood
as if you were a shepherd

You
with the white Impala
broken driver's side back seat window
covered with a Hefty bag

You
with your back-bedroom window
wearing a wrap of aluminum foil

You
who walk to the convenience store with bars on the windows
bare-chested, shirt in hand
trailing like a broken wing

You
who bring back beer and pork rinds
and a single orange to your momma
who sits on your springless couch
and complains about how, oh Lordy, how much
her feet ache from a long shift at the chicken plant

You
who dump the dog's big plastic water bowl
and fill it with hot water and three tablespoons of salt
and lower her swollen feet into the heat

You
kneeling, with a towel draped over your shoulder
dry one wet foot, then the other
and Momma says you are just like Jesus from that story

You
who say, "Jesus, Momma"
but don't mean the same thing.

Patients

At the doctor's office waiting room
the stubborn summer rain
chatters against the windows
gathers into narrow streams of liquid tongues
lapping at the glass. Still, a woman has started humming
then quietly singing, "This Little Light of Mine."
She sits next to a man with broomstick arms
patched with gauze in the crooks of his elbows—
signs of recent bloodlettings, or driplines, or both.

I am waiting for my wife to return
from the inner chambers of the heart clinic;
and here, in my exile, seated next to a lonely rack
of thumb-worn magazines, a Styrofoam cup of cold coffee
useless in my hand, I can't for the life of me
remember what that little light is
the woman only four chairs over softly sings about.

Grackles at the Stoplight

At the intersection of Garriott and Cleveland streets
by the big Walmart, crosswise from Atwood's
(if you know the town)

grackles roam the aisle of car grills
to pick the teeth of our machines
like egrets along a rhino's smile.

They value the mostly mangled
radiator roasted, wind dried
heat toughened, dirt seasoned—

grasshoppers, the yellow ones of late summer
or the leafy tinged katydid
the palm-sized lunar moth

with their frightening false eyes
the monarchs come back from
Mexico, interrupted in their migration.

The birds know our frantic habits
and in their bird wisdom
know we come and go

having collided with lives
we didn't even notice.

III

this late in harvest time

September Matins

It is morning

but too late to build
an altar of stone, you say,

or a fire for offerings, I say.

We laugh at ourselves
and talk in the driveway.

>	Venus hangs
>	a silver pendant
>	from the horns
>	of the waning moon.

We settle for a wordless hymn
of measured breath and upward gaze
at lunar crown and ashen jewel.

Testing Protagoras
Of all things the measure is man—Protagoras

In early October the Big Dipper
stands on its handle in my front yard
balanced on the chin of the northern horizon—
a carnival trick of a cosmic juggler.
Westward, Cassiopeia tilts on her head
cold Grecian robes bunched around her elegant shoulders
those W-shaped stars a glimmer of silver brooches.

An upside-down queen and a ladle eternally suspended
an arm's length apart, but not even angels could close that
distance in a million years, and God could not balance
long enough in the field of time on the ball of His right foot
to take one single step across an abyss as that.
Yet when I raise my arm to the sky, a mere cubit in measure,
elbow touches cold steel, knuckles bury in a fold of gown.

6 AM

The cats are awake
and giving chase—
sometimes to each other
sometimes to thin air.

The dogs, who sleep later,
stir in their round doggie beds
yawn like dads
after a nap.

My wife is buried
in sheets and pillows
shields and shells
of fabric and stuffing

as if to fend off
what is coming—
and what is coming
sounds its first footfalls

on the porch slats
which creak cold
under its gray weight—
the light not far behind.

My Mother's Revision

She said she thought they were just leaves blowing across the road, a motley crew of Sycamore rinds, gloves of yellow and gold skipping in a rowdy row. It reminded her, she said, of when I raced across the backyard and buried myself in the raked pile, scattering all that hard work, and came out wearing a prickly wig that dismembered in the wind. It wasn't until she saw the tiny explosions of feathers in the rear-view mirror that she knew the moving shapes were quail scurrying from cover.

And in her mind, lately filled with the debris of dementia, in that reconsidered memory, I bury myself again and again in that mound of piling thoughts where I will remain hidden and safe until spring, or long thereafter.

Feeding My Mother an Enchilada

When she was on her fifth and final confinement at the hospital
and my father had fallen asleep in the corner chair
a nurse came with a tray of lunch
under what looked like an orange hubcap.
I lifted the lid, and my mother, who couldn't remember my name,
said, "Enchiladas."

I unwrapped the fork and knife,
then tucked a paper napkin into the neck of her gown.
I poured Sprite into a Styrofoam cup of ice.

What strange egg hatched this flightless adult?
What addled neurons had tipped and fractured
so she couldn't lift her arms
or remember all her children's names?

While my father rested distant in his slumber, I rolled my sleeves
above the elbows, carved an inch of enchilada,
raised the morsel with a fork, and asked her to "Open up"
just as she had prodded me more than 50 years earlier,
a fledgling flapping in a high chair,
her sitting at the kitchen table, holding a fork, saying,
"One more bite. Just one last bite."

On My 58th Birthday
for E.C. Bowers, Jr.

My eighty-nine-year-old father says when I was born
the doctor pronounced me a baby boy
big enough to push a wheelbarrow.

Wood handles worn smooth to shine,
arms aching, legs quivering
but we're both still pushing
      aren't we, Old Man?—

our barrows overfilled with all we've gathered,
behind us a trail of cobbled losses.

The time will come when--
the cart too full to budge--
you'll ask me to finish the job.

I'll oblige, lift with my knees
as you taught me to do
empty all that needs emptying between us.

Come evening
you'll take up the lighter handles
steer for the darkening shed.

Running in the Dark

I wear a chest strap with a round light
a glowing heart like Iron Man
only my light is yellowish
like a headlight off an old Impala.

I wonder what the neighbor thinks
the one half mile down the road
who is up before daybreak
to spike his round bales
and feed his cattle?

He sits at his kitchen table
pressed next to the window
work-rough finger curled round the handle of a coffee cup
a last fork of scrambled egg
and half a biscuit with marmalade
on his plate

when that distant light appears
a slow-moving dim flame
a nodding ball of pale energy.

Maybe a drunk on a motorcycle?
Maybe a one-eyed car with a flat tire?
Maybe a spirit risen from the nearby cemetery
the one that butts up against his north pasture?
Maybe a raccoon caught on fire?—
which seems unlikely but not entirely impossible—

no more impossible than a sixty-year-old
jogging before sunrise
along a deeply rural road
fearful of ankle-wrenching ruts
snakes, low-hanging limbs,
imagined dangers lurking in the shadows

or just the fear of being unseen
by a farmer pulling out of his drive
half-asleep in the morning blackness.

Late Harvest

My garden space
is a discarded horse trough
burr-lipped, oblong
wearing a skirt of rust
that weeps into a reddened hem.
Its internal organs
a carnival of filler—
a stomach of driftwood
two lungs of red brick
a colon of knotted garden hose
oak limbs its bones
dirt its flesh and porous skin.

Something still grows there
late in this dying year—
reddened peppers are
its pointy toes
brown tomato vines
its writhing hair
the eggplant
a purple bladder ballooned
with God knows what
yellow squash
the jaundiced fingers
of a drunk.

I hesitate behind the screen door
this late in harvest time
feel in my own body
lightened of its summer life
the shorter season to come.

IV

the long winter of memory

Origin Story

The moon is a mottled ball of snow
tossed into the sky a few billion years ago

by a boy who rolled it in his cold
reddened palms, then launched it toward his sister.

The whitened moon arcs across the sky in eternal parabola—
while Sister ducks behind a nebula hedge,

eyes closed, giggling,
the round revenge of interstellar dust in hand.

Two Photos

the tree I photographed
one winter
extends an ice-encrusted limb
along the top rail
of the pipe and cable fence
like the arm of a lover
over the shoulder of the beloved

in another photo
taken after a deep snow
the dog, a Great Pyrenees,
is a snowwoman come to life

one died before the other
the tree and the dog
though we don't recall
which went first, which last

yet they hang
only a few inches apart
in the long winter of memory
on a wall
we haven't painted in years.

In the Pocket of My Winter Coat

Sometimes I reach into my coat pocket
and pull out an apple
full and comfortable in its autumn skin.

Sometimes what I pull from my coat pocket is less a sphere
more curvaceous, like a pear
soft and broad-hipped.

Sometimes it is a small angry stone
smoothed by time, guilt-ridden, careworn
and ready to be thrown.

Sometimes I retrieve an earth
spinning slowly in my palm, lands and oceans held so tightly
by gravity, my hand stays clean and dry.

Sometimes it's a warm moon I hold in both hands
like the cradled face of a child
full and reflective of another's light.

Sometimes my hand dips into a cold cavern of emptiness
where I find the pocket-lint of passing stars
and space in all its shapelessness.

Spooky Action at a Distance

The calf
a meringue bull-to-be

stares through thick molasses eyes

at his strange complement
beyond the pipe-and-cable fence.

I stare back, as humans do,
a mirrored particle of sorts

and wonder what subtle entanglements
have already passed between those taut strands

to hold us suspended
in this pastured space.

Drinking Beer and Writing Poetry

What off-rhymes may come.
                What oxymorons
and mixed metaphors.

        What misspellings
inexact meters
and oddly
broken
        lines.

Let the words stumble
across the page
        like a carouser's
late-night tracks
                in snow:

        dactylic footfalls
anapestic stutters
end-stopped lines teetering
                near the margin's gutter.

Oh, let the words drop
        where they may,
                let them flop
upon their backs
        and carve in snow

the wide tippling wings
of a fallen muse
        singing some ancient
        brewer's tune.

Body and Soul

We want to know those last words
just before the transition to corpse

waiting here on the material side
of the dual divide of brain and mind,

body and soul.
And we want to know

who's waiting just across the border
hoping for a whisper over the shoulder

before the voice finally goes
before the eyes fill with weeds

and lips turn to stone.
I offer you this invitation:

Come closer at that moment.
Lean over. I'll say it out loud for all to hear.

Holy shit! I'll declare,
They'll print it in the local paper,

next to the weekly Sheriff's Report.
Surely in the obituaries.

Better yet, it's Sunday bulletin material,
or worthy of a banner slung from the tail

of a circling biplane. Holy Shit! fluttering across the sky,
and you'll wonder, all of you,

until that moment of your own,
exactly what I meant by it.

Birthdays There

In heaven party balloons
never lose their helium.

The cake bleached angelic white
will never grow stale, or ever be sliced
and eaten.

There will be endless punch
spiked and unspiked

and gifts in perpetual wrappings
and bows.

Those invited stand with glasses raised
and salute the fact
of their missing lives.

The decay of winter
is all they have lost, they say,
and the painful turnings of the years

yet they each make a secret wish
and try to blow the candles out.

December

While the horses
dishevel
the round hay bale

a winter fog rides
careless
upon their backs

until a mid-morning
breeze
unsaddles the mist

and those ragged souls,
upended, depart.

Season's Greetings

A raccoon corpse partly covered in snow
at the edge of the road is a festive reminder
of the coming holiday season. The long slow
rot of fall, the year, an old man by now, balanced
on the edge of a cliff until the hard knuckle of winter
lands a blow on his stubbled chin and sends him
tumbling in fluttering leaves, like molted turkey feathers
and it is the last we will see of him for a while.

A worker from the county Department of Transportation
will pull up in a white Chevy pickup before nightfall
take a shovel from the bed, slide the frozen raccoon
into a white five-gallon bucket.

When he removes his Mule gloves
tosses them back onto the cluttered dash
he'll think how good the warm air feels blowing from the vents
and he'll think of his wife at home
who is just beginning to consider details of Christmas dinner
when the kids are out of school
and the snow lies clean and taut as a bedsheet
along the shoulder of the highway, again.

The Sky Rests in Pure Blue Thought

The sky rests in pure blue thought.
Clouds are rumors on the far horizon.
Even the birds have cleared the air.

The red ants who built a domed colony
near the edge of the road
have long left off foraging
and gone underground for the season.

For a brief moment
I stand on the porch
emptied of all sorrows
and the thought we are out of milk and bread
with snow on the way.

Then I remember.

Formal Complaint

The guy with a Santa beard
drunk on gin
tells the cops at his door
someone is sneaking around
his backyard
and maybe
wants to kill him.

Or maybe
it's his old lady
who left him
right after the holidays
finally come round
for her clothes
and needlepoint bag.

Or maybe
it's some cold-weather animal
hoofing around in the dark.

Or maybe
it's the rowdy children next door
he once brought into his workshop
and taught how to use a drill and saw
then they stole beer and sandwich meat
from his Sears upright.

The cops take the complaint
they'll later throw away.

If he had to make a definitive list,
no one—
not his old lady
not the town cops
not the neighbor kids—
believes in him anymore.

Elegy for Donald Hall
    "In order to write it, you cannot be aware of the second part."
                                                            DH (1928-2018)

Jane was the hymnic bard
while you were the North-
easterner, the Yankee full blown.
I came to share in your
sufferings when you lost her.

I watched your lives together
a dozen dozen times over:
you, clean shaven then,
hair cut short and stark. I heard
her tell of her depression

and of your bouts with cancer.
And from you I learned
that a poem moves both north
and south, that the good ones,
unmeasured by the poet's compass,

drift in their own mystical directions.
I have no ghostly blue mountain
no looming Mt. Kearsarge
only wheat fields, blue sky
too much rain, or too little rain

but I understood your vision
and I understood her praise
and the love of words
that passed between you—
hers into yours, yours into hers.

The Making of Poetry

I have had
Poems form

Like breath
Condensed on glass.

—

Other times
Born of despair

They pour
Like lead into bullet molds.

—

I have carpentered letters
Into syllables

Tongue-and-grooved words
Into phrases

Box nailed sentences
Into stanzas.

—

Sometimes
A hand intervenes

Delicate
As a child's

To crayon secret shapes
And almost words.

Those
I magnet

To the fridge
To be read

By the shadow
Of my mother
Who slippers into the kitchen
At midnight and

Hungry for something
Turns on the light.

On My Father Dying Behind Hospital Glass

1.

My father is dying behind the glass
air hose attached to his mask
tended by a nurse in deep sea diver's suit.

2.

My father is dying in an aquarium.
You aren't supposed to
tap on the glass
but I tap
and tap and tap again
hoping to change his direction
like a fish turned from a hook.

3.

My father is dying on the sea floor.
I look on
from a glass-bottom boat.

4.

My father is dying in a sunken submarine.
If I had a wrench I'd bang out "H-a-n-g o-n" in Morse code—
but it's too late, it's been too long
and he is fathoms deep.

Osteomancy

Of all the things you left us
when you died
thank you, Dad,
for the bag of keys

that satchel of metal bones
we rattle through our fingers
looking for the one

that unlocks your toolbox
or starts the riding mower
releases the chain
from the pasture gate
wakes up the tractor
fits the back door
the side door
or a door you no longer had.

We cast the collection across
your kitchen table
hope to divine what fits what.

There are more keys than locks
more questions than answers.

We wonder what else you knew
or want to tell us
but keep to yourself.

My Neighbor Tells Me About Losing Her Father

He asked to be turned to ashes
[she says]
to avoid the expense
of a long-term relationship
with the crooked American Cemetery Association.
He was frugal that way.

When we brought him home
we put him on the highest shelf
where the cats couldn't reach.
He claimed to be a dog person—
an outright lie given the number of cats.

That spring, we divided him into smaller portions
scattered some over mountains, and some in the sea,
even though he was afraid of heights, and couldn't swim.
But he wanted the adventure, you know?

I read in a magazine a person sheds 40,000 skin cells a minute.
He lived with us for over twenty years
so sometimes when I empty the vacuum cleaner
or sweep the kitchen floor, I worry about that.

He's been gone awhile now, though,
so I'm not as careful as I used to be
with my routine cleaning chores.

Driving by Our Old, Abandoned House

My brother and sisters have long moved elsewhere.
Mom and Dad have vanished as well
with no hope of coming back
to settle into their favorite reading chairs
set opposite sides of the living room—
her to live in her romances
him his westerns.

I don't get out of the car
or even park in the crumbling driveway.
Instead I drive slowly by
to salvage what is salvageable:

the long-gone dogs and cats
sweet tea, cornbread
bunkbeds, birthday bicycles
report cards, good and bad
a broken tooth from an uncaught baseball
an old church piano, a stringless guitar
Christmas trees too anemic to hold their ornaments
but also a garden once so full of okra and melons
the neighbors stopped opening their doors.

I can't drive slowly enough to save any more.

A Short Bucket List of Impossible Things

1. Learn to levitate
2. Grow back my wisdom teeth
3. Capture and release a Passenger pigeon
4. Talk to my great-great-great-great grandmother, Mary Lincoln Stover
5. Pick up that sack of empty beer cans I tossed out the truck window on County Line Road, 44 years ago
6. Take back the bullet that killed that quietly moving doe
7. Ask Jesus who he really thought he was
8. and based on his answer, decide what to do next

Golden-tongued

In El Bahnasa, Egypt
a man, woman, a three-year old
were mummified two millennia ago
with tongues of gold leaf in their mouths
so given the power to speak
to Osiris in the afterlife.

We set off on our routine journeys
with words in our mouths to say what we need to say
to each other—
ordinary utterances to our ordinary gods

so when you announce it is time to go to the grocery store
I say, I'm ready, pick up my keys
and follow you out the door.

Nearly There

It is complete

    when the sun sets

    the snow melts

the plate is cleaned of vegetables

the radio is tuned to silence

    the final drop of something hits the ground

    the chair creaks when risen from

the tomb empties when risen from

the cliff ends as all cliffs do

    while the sea churns below

    our ears deafened by those cold deep waters.

County Road 48

I have travelled this simple road
10,000 miles and more

at a walk, a jog, a run

behind the wheel
or in the passenger seat

saddled to a reluctant horse
and one more willing

I have circumnavigated
half the globe

repeating this stretch
of gravel and sand

made it a fair distance
into the lower heavens

witnessed the moon rounder
and fresher of face

eastward, Venus and the corner post
mark the morning's start

westward, the falling sun
a spider's thread, the finish line.

After the Storm

Once the ice storm has passed
there remains the task
of gathering the glazed broken limbs.

Some are too large to drag
so with chainsaw, and in full sight of the ice-shocked
trees, the elephantine limbs are cut
into cow and sheep length ulnas
then gurneyed by awkward wheelbarrow
to the growing charnel chaos of the brush pile.

From there, rabbits will emerge slim and muscled
in spring.

www.ingramcontent.com/pod-product-compliance
Lightning Source LLC
Chambersburg PA
CBHW020547080526
44583CB00013B/1034